MAKE CHANGES

Make Changes

Written by: Dan L. Franklin

Copyright © 2023 by Franklin Speaks Up

All rights reserved. No part of this book shall be reproduced, stored in a retrieval system, or transmitted by any means, electronic, mechanical, photocopying, recording, or otherwise, without written permission from the publisher. No patent liability is assumed with respect to the use of the information contained herein. Although every precaution has been taken of this book, the publisher and author assume no responsibility for errors or omissions. Nor is any liability assumed for damages resulting from the use of the information contained herein.

ISBN# 979-8-218-05767-1
Library of Congress Cataloging-in-Publishing in process
Printed in the United States of America

First Printing: May, 2023
Warning and Disclaimer

The information provided is on an "as is" basis. The author and the publisher shall have neither liability nor responsibility to any person or entity with respect to any loss or damages arising from the information contained in this book or from the use of its thoughts.

Feedback: feedback@franklinspeaksup.com
Bulk Sales: bulksales@franklinspeaksup.com

ALWAYS HAVE GOOD INTENTIONS

www.franklinspeaksup.com

About the Author/Introduction

Several years ago, Dan L. Franklin, (aka Franklin) experienced many life challenges and changes that catapulted him to think about his Tough Struggle.

During this period Franklin went through a bitter divorce, he lost his father at 59 to colon cancer, and his mother she was 66 to a very rare blood disease (TTP) Thrombocytopenic Purpura. In addition, Franklin was subjected to a mountain of lies, deceit, manipulation and many threats.

Franklin has a Series 3 license, he successfully passed the CPA exam, and later became Diversity Team Leader and Sr. Director/Vice President of Sponsorships with the American Express Company.

Prior to the American Express Company, Franklin was an outstanding commodities broker. As a top ten commodities broker gave Franklin the opportunity to travel around the world meeting people in all walks of life.

As an accountant with one of the largest CPA firms in the world, he served as the tax accountant for the late great *Muhammad Ali*.

After several losses of love, wealth, and recovery inspired Franklin to entrepreneurship. Today, Franklin is an author, mentor & life coach empowering social change.

(continue on next page)

About the Author/Introduction

Knowing an autobiography might thwart his aspiration for getting his message to those wanting self-empowerment, and thinking through their life`s journey. Franklin began writing snippets of thoughts that resonated with him daily. Sometimes, stagnating his very moments.

In his new book, *"Make Changes,"* Franklin believed that writing powerful but simple thoughts that make change might be the empowerment others needed to, "Make Changes".

ALWAYS HAVE GOOD INTENTIONS

Contents

Written by..2
About Author 3
Make Changes..5 – 261
In Closing 263

ALWAYS HAVE GOOD INTENTIONS

MAKE CHANGES

always have good intentions

by

Dan L. Franklin

Be kind, creative, daring, positive, loving, humble, committed, confident, honest, brave, optimistic, grateful, thankful, and happy.

MAKE CHANGES

Always be in charge of your happiness.

ALWAYS HAVE GOOD INTENTIONS

Are you sitting in your choices?

*If you believe,
you will have success.*

MAKE CHANGES

*Don't try to be,
what you are not.*

ALWAYS HAVE GOOD INTENTIONS

MAKE CHANGES

Everyone has a voice.

ALWAYS HAVE GOOD INTENTIONS

Teacher, Student or Both?

Tolerance allows the freedom of choice and the opinions of others.

Define Respect.

MAKE CHANGES

There are two kinds of trust;

You trusting others, and others trusting you.

ALWAYS HAVE GOOD INTENTIONS

MAKE CHANGES

A mind which is unsettled is easily influenced.

ALWAYS HAVE GOOD INTENTIONS

MAKE CHANGES

Always Have Good Intentions.

MAKE CHANGES

Spend time with yourself.

MAKE CHANGES

You are most vulnerable to whom you love and trust.

ALWAYS HAVE GOOD INTENTIONS

If your life is consumed with trying to "discredit" someone,

you have "nothing" to offer anyone.

MAKE CHANGES

Can you see their goodness?

ALWAYS HAVE GOOD INTENTIONS

MAKE CHANGES

Closed ears will blind you.

ALWAYS HAVE GOOD INTENTIONS

MAKE CHANGES

Bitterness is poison

Push back gently.

MAKE CHANGES

Your lies belong to you!

Enjoy what you know.

MAKE CHANGES

Building friendships will always take time.

ALWAYS HAVE GOOD INTENTIONS

*Financially prepare
at the beginning for the end.*

You can't change something you worship.

Feeling sorry for yourself is the prelude to depression.

*Stop giving
your choices away.*

There are four components of success;

Time, Process, Discipline and Commitment.

MAKE CHANGES

Learn to apologize,

it's like learning to forgive.

ALWAYS HAVE GOOD INTENTIONS

Dishonesty will escort you to the gutter.

MAKE CHANGES

Do something,

                          Give something

Love something

                     Share something,

Build something.

MAKE CHANGES

*Be careful when you speak,
"your ears" are listening.*

ALWAYS HAVE GOOD INTENTIONS

So many people are conditioned to hearing lies,

they don't know when they're being told the truth.

So tell the truth, because they'll think you're lying anyway.

I can see, I can hear,
I can walk, and I can talk.

Which one can you do without?

What's the difference between a con, a thief, and a liar?

Try to listen without judgement to someone who's looking for your attention.

MAKE CHANGES

*Anger and Hate
is like poison, and expecting the
other person to die.*

MAKE CHANGES

Work isn't always hard.

MAKE CHANGES

Read what you need to know.

&

Write what you need to say.

Don't be afraid to change, it's required of everyone.

*The root of a problem
is where every problem is solved.*

*Living life is the ability to challenge yourself beyond all the things
you think you know.*

MAKE CHANGES

Denial is deadly,

&

emotionally damaging.

ALWAYS HAVE GOOD INTENTIONS

Learn your purpose.

MAKE CHANGES

Keeping secrets will cost you something.

ALWAYS HAVE GOOD INTENTIONS

MAKE CHANGES

Why is your behavior the same everyday?

ALWAYS HAVE GOOD INTENTIONS

MAKE CHANGES

Your purpose! Your life!

Unconditional love is unconditional.

MAKE CHANGES

Breaking a habit,

is just a decision away.

Knowing one side of a story attempts to keep all "lies" safe.

Knowing both sides of the story tends to remove deceit and manipulation,

and will bring you closer to the truth, if not the truth.

Your gift has always been in front of you, so pay attention.

What's personal to you,

is personal to you.

MAKE CHANGES

*You gave 100% participation.
But, did you?*

ALWAYS HAVE GOOD INTENTIONS

MAKE CHANGES

Taking ownership of your decisions nurtures accountability, responsibility, and growth.

MAKE CHANGES

Know your "kryptonite".

MAKE CHANGES

*When you have given up,
your heart and your soul
is the first to know.*

ALWAYS HAVE GOOD INTENTIONS

Why do you expect to receive, and never give?

MAKE CHANGES

When you have decided who you are, stay strong, and keep moving forward.

MAKE CHANGES

*Individuality
is very special, treasure it.*

ALWAYS HAVE GOOD INTENTIONS

Always check yourself with yourself and keep it 100.

ALWAYS HAVE GOOD INTENTIONS

Living life is always learning.

If you love someone at the beginning of a relationship,

and hated them at the end of the relationship,

you should question whether you loved them at all.

Understand the words you have chosen to voice, before you speak.

MAKE CHANGES

Why do you expect success?

ALWAYS HAVE GOOD INTENTIONS

MAKE CHANGES

Everything you do matters.

ALWAYS HAVE GOOD INTENTIONS

You want to be heard?

I want to be heard too.

What's your purpose?

If you have nothing positive to say, why say anything at all?

MAKE CHANGES

A nasty disposition will close every door you think you have opened.

ALWAYS HAVE GOOD INTENTIONS

A person who never learns, will always have challenges they could have avoided.

MAKE CHANGES

Why are you yelling?

ALWAYS HAVE GOOD INTENTIONS

Everything you need starts and stops with you.

Conversations may begin with differences.

MAKE CHANGES

Don't be a hypocrite.

What's the difference between

a

control freak and a narcissi?

MAKE CHANGES

The hardest part of being focused,
is staying focused.

ALWAYS HAVE GOOD INTENTIONS

Without your health, your family, friends, and haters will miss you.

When you begin to understand living life is a lot like politics, (you can't please everyone), then and only then will you succeed.

*Jealous people
will always be sad people.*

*They spend time in your
business, because they have no
business
of their own.*

Stay away from them.

MAKE CHANGES

Double Dealer.

Good? Not so Good?

MAKE CHANGES

Why lie to me, I was there.

ALWAYS HAVE GOOD INTENTIONS

*Mistakes and Failures
are no less
than growth, and growth
is no more than learning.*

MAKE CHANGES

*Your ability to embrace
differences in others is what
validates
your uniqueness
and
outstanding qualities.*

ALWAYS HAVE GOOD INTENTIONS

I know you have something to say, so speak up.

MAKE CHANGES

Sometimes, when our hearts open, our eyes leak.

When your life appears to be upside down, it's not.

Simply put, a challenge is in front of you.

Live a lie or live the truth, can't decide?

Make Changes!

MAKE CHANGES

Your integrity will determine your honesty.

ALWAYS HAVE GOOD INTENTIONS

MAKE CHANGES

Will you keep wondering who you are?

ALWAYS HAVE GOOD INTENTIONS

MAKE CHANGES

If you can't judge yourself, what's the point of judging others?

ALWAYS HAVE GOOD INTENTIONS

MAKE CHANGES

What is your commitment?

MAKE CHANGES

Some people are forever bitter, stop trying to please them.

In fact, leave them alone.

MAKE CHANGES

Your will to succeed must out-weigh your arrogance.

If your chase is money your greed will get you.

If your chase is revenge your ego will fail you.

MAKE CHANGES

If your conversation with someone can't encourage them to keep moving forward, be silent.

ALWAYS HAVE GOOD INTENTIONS

Take time to be patient, grateful and quiet.

MAKE CHANGES

*Being at peace
with every decision
allows the self to grow.*

MAKE CHANGES

*I never fell out of love,
I just made a different decision.*

MAKE CHANGES

Believe it or not, everything you do has a process!

Goals, obligations, responsibilities, commitments, setbacks, are all attributes of growth and life moving forward.

MAKE CHANGES

Are you someone's miracle?

ALWAYS HAVE GOOD INTENTIONS

MAKE CHANGES

*When you decide to
give your option(s) away,
don't get upset when
the outcome is not in your favor.*

ALWAYS HAVE GOOD INTENTIONS
www.franklinspeaksup.com

MAKE CHANGES

Would you change places with someone who was hurting?

ALWAYS HAVE GOOD INTENTIONS

MAKE CHANGES

*In order to advance
you must be open to change.*

MAKE CHANGES

Your belief in yourself is not required, it's mandatory.

MAKE CHANGES

Denial will never allow you to be honest with yourself.

MAKE CHANGES

*The promises you make to others
is just as important as*

*the promises
you make to yourself.*

ALWAYS HAVE GOOD INTENTIONS

*Know what you know,
and allow others
to know what they know.*

Maybe together we can grow.

Your beauty is within your soul, not what's on your feet.

MAKE CHANGES

You will always be stretched and forever judged.

Lying is the obvious form of dishonesty.

MAKE CHANGES

Your day starts when you start, and stops when you stop.

ALWAYS HAVE GOOD INTENTIONS

MAKE CHANGES

You don't have to debate or remember what you said,

if you told the truth.

ALWAYS HAVE GOOD INTENTIONS

Detachment is the power to remain free from the influences of others, if you wish to keep yourself grounded.

*Never fear the truth,
the truth will keep you safe.*

MAKE CHANGES

It's not your fault.

ALWAYS HAVE GOOD INTENTIONS

MAKE CHANGES

Are assumptions just another opinion?

ALWAYS HAVE GOOD INTENTIONS

MAKE CHANGES

Without wisdom, we tend to make decisions that challenge us.

ALWAYS HAVE GOOD INTENTIONS

MAKE CHANGES

There is one thing I know we all have in common, and that is time.

But, how we spend our time is what separates us.

MAKE CHANGES

Your love for others must show up in yourself first.

ALWAYS HAVE GOOD INTENTIONS

Your choice.

Your decision.

MAKE CHANGES

When you decide, is when a decision has been made.

ALWAYS HAVE GOOD INTENTIONS

Having goals in life is what gives living texture.

*If you surround yourself daily
with people and stuff
that make you happy,*

*you will witness
a positive shift in you.*

MAKE CHANGES

Make a conscious decision

to live in the past

or

the present.

ALWAYS HAVE GOOD INTENTIONS

We all have opinions.

*Just don't get caught up
in the translation.*

MAKE CHANGES

When you believe in yourself and possibilities, don't be surprised when things you do seem effortless.

No Homework, No Research, More Mistakes.

MAKE CHANGES

Recognize and acknowledge of your blessings out loud.

ALWAYS HAVE GOOD INTENTIONS

You will become how you behave.

Your stories both past and present will build character, if you pay attention.

Love "as is".

Have grace under pressure.

Always Believe in Yourself.

Who will determine

my truth, you?

Learn how to pick yourself up.

MAKE CHANGES

Guilt belongs to...

Success is a result of thinking that way!

MAKE CHANGES

*There are
bad mothers & bad fathers,*

which one are you?

MAKE CHANGES

Did you ask the question?

ALWAYS HAVE GOOD INTENTIONS

Without wisdom we tend to speak before we gather our thoughts.

Race will always matter, until it does not!

MAKE CHANGES

How do you challenge something you know nothing about?

If you ask someone a question, and an answer is given to a question you did not ask, its probably safe to say;

They don't have an answer, or the answer they gave, keeps them from telling a lie to your question.

MAKE CHANGES

I know the truth hurts sometimes.

Just keep it on push.

MAKE CHANGES

Your happiness will always be your responsibility.

MAKE CHANGES

Create a friendship with yourself, and bond with your soul.

MAKE CHANGES

*You do know time,
will never stand still for you.*

ALWAYS HAVE GOOD INTENTIONS

*Sin is Sin,
what's yours?*

Have you ever been invited to a pity party?

Don't go!

MAKE CHANGES

What is a deadbeat?

Never panic.

MAKE CHANGES

Wisdom is waiting for you at the finish line.

ALWAYS HAVE GOOD INTENTIONS

You can't expect to take and never give.

MAKE CHANGES

*Do you listen,
as much as you talk?*

The magic happens when you believe!

MAKE CHANGES

*May your life
be as you planned it,*

if you planned it.

ALWAYS HAVE GOOD INTENTIONS

Stop wasting time!

Make Changes

MAKE CHANGES

Are you okay?

MAKE CHANGES

Your ability to understand who you are, will allow self to make changes.

MAKE CHANGES

Your denial will determine your addiction.

Why so complicated?

MAKE CHANGES

Any form of negativity is evil.

ALWAYS HAVE GOOD INTENTIONS

Trust is always necessary if you want to help.

MAKE CHANGES

Kindness requires no money.

MAKE CHANGES

People that lie and remain bitter are stuck in denial, let them be.

ALWAYS HAVE GOOD INTENTIONS

MAKE CHANGES

Let your thoughts be heard.

Drama is like cancer, it will suck the life right out of you.

MAKE CHANGES

*Did you know,
every time you hear good news
you have just been blessed?*

ALWAYS HAVE GOOD INTENTIONS

Are you living life on purpose or by accident?

MAKE CHANGES

Does losing or winning really matter?

Happiness is the only measuring stick

MAKE CHANGES

Be forgiving!

*Without women,
men would not exist.*

*Ok they disappoint us, but we
disappoint them too!*

Stay in the present.

MAKE CHANGES

Never speak for someone else.

ALWAYS HAVE GOOD INTENTIONS

Spend the time you need to understand a subject matter, not to memorize it.

MAKE CHANGES

*If your life is defined by lies,
what kind of life are you living?*

ALWAYS HAVE GOOD INTENTIONS
www.franklinspeaksup.com

MAKE CHANGES

Your accomplishments will depend on your ability to manage emotional threats.

MAKE CHANGES

Are your dreams worth your time?

ALWAYS HAVE GOOD INTENTIONS

*You should know
money follows, it does not lead.*

MAKE CHANGES

Being in GOOD health allows you to participate in life's journey.

MAKE CHANGES

Isn't your baggage enough to manage?

ALWAYS HAVE GOOD INTENTIONS

MAKE CHANGES

You can't fix a relationship or anything else with bad intentions.

ALWAYS HAVE GOOD INTENTIONS

Your lifestyle belongs to your choices.

MAKE CHANGES

You will always be learning,

so take a seat.

ALWAYS HAVE GOOD INTENTIONS

*How do you breathe
inside out or outside in?*

MAKE CHANGES

Manifestation is alive and well, so be mindful of what you think about.

ALWAYS HAVE GOOD INTENTIONS

MAKE CHANGES

Sometimes its required to react from the soul when drawn in by the flesh.

*We all teach,
but do we all listen?*

MAKE CHANGES

If you won't decide, I will.

ALWAYS HAVE GOOD INTENTIONS

MAKE CHANGES

Unconditional love is the ability to love unconditionally.

Face it!

MAKE CHANGES

Integrity

Honesty

Kindness

Respect

Loyalty

Wisdom

Have these values left the building?

ALWAYS HAVE GOOD INTENTIONS

MAKE CHANGES

*How do you value
what you know?*

ALWAYS HAVE GOOD INTENTIONS

MAKE CHANGES

Your life's direction depends on what seeds you have planted

or what seeds others have planted for you.

ALWAYS HAVE GOOD INTENTIONS

MAKE CHANGES

You can avoid depression.

ALWAYS HAVE GOOD INTENTIONS
201
www.franklinspeaksup.com

MAKE CHANGES

Stay away from the rabbit hole.

*Pay attention
to the road you have chosen.*

MAKE CHANGES

Belief and Passion is not to be confused with Ego and Arrogance.

MAKE CHANGES

Is denial a friend of yours?

ALWAYS HAVE GOOD INTENTIONS

MAKE CHANGES

Your will must be managed, and your spirit must be free to live.

MAKE CHANGES

How do you decide if Black Lives Matters to you?

ALWAYS HAVE GOOD INTENTIONS

MAKE CHANGES

How do you listen?

ALWAYS HAVE GOOD INTENTIONS

Do you have a need to trust?

Make Changes

MAKE CHANGES

Relationships are built on mutual trust and interest.

ALWAYS HAVE GOOD INTENTIONS

MAKE CHANGES

Say Hello.

MAKE CHANGES

Your thoughts are just as important as your focus.

ALWAYS HAVE GOOD INTENTIONS

MAKE CHANGES

Can you identify your blessings from yesterday?

ALWAYS HAVE GOOD INTENTIONS

Leave the drama alone, it will destroy the soul.

MAKE CHANGES

No seeds, No fruit.

MAKE CHANGES

Toxic?

Make Changes!

ALWAYS HAVE GOOD INTENTIONS

MAKE CHANGES

Volunteer to help yourself change.

MAKE CHANGES

What you believe may not be accurate.

MAKE CHANGES

Never give up on you.

ALWAYS HAVE GOOD INTENTIONS

MAKE CHANGES

The revolution happens when the powerful believe they are not require to answer to,

"We the People"

Curse your kids, get cursed back.

Why expect anything more?

MAKE CHANGES

Disrespect, means no respect.

ALWAYS HAVE GOOD INTENTIONS

Trust feeds the mind, while distrust destroys it.

MAKE CHANGES

Do you see yourself from the inside out or from the outside in?

*Is interpretation
a matter of perception?*

MAKE CHANGES

When you look in the mirror who do you see?

*It's okay to treasure
how different you are.*

MAKE CHANGES

Sometimes we look, we know, and don't act.

ALWAYS HAVE GOOD INTENTIONS

*No father? No mother?
But, plenty of love.*

MAKE CHANGES

Tell me, you didn't know.

Why settle for what is expected of you?

MAKE CHANGES

Trust until you can't.

You can't run away from being who you are.

MAKE CHANGES

I prefer to grow with you.

Will I? Can I?

ALWAYS HAVE GOOD INTENTIONS

MAKE CHANGES

Your GOD lives deep inside of you.

Pay Attention!

ALWAYS HAVE GOOD INTENTIONS

MAKE CHANGES

Sometimes it's required you change your way of life.

MAKE CHANGES

Nothing but LOVE.

ALWAYS HAVE GOOD INTENTIONS

Show up.

The visual self should always be on point.

MAKE CHANGES

Lies, deceit, disrespect, manipulation and drama will destroy the children.

MAKE CHANGES

What consumes your life?

Have we gotten so un-attached, that we are afraid to help one another?

MAKE CHANGES

You need you, not me.

ALWAYS HAVE GOOD INTENTIONS

MAKE CHANGES

Stop disrespecting yourself, and build something.

MAKE CHANGES

Should I care about you, if you don't care about you?

MAKE CHANGES

I know you have something to say, so speak up!

ALWAYS HAVE GOOD INTENTIONS

Some decisions are difficult.
But, one has to be made.

MAKE CHANGES

We need each other more than you know.

ALWAYS HAVE GOOD INTENTIONS

MAKE CHANGES

Your dreams will be fulfilled when you are consumed by them.

ALWAYS HAVE GOOD INTENTIONS

Work harder?

Quit?

or

Make Changes?

MAKE CHANGES

Your anger comes from the inability to understand why you are really upset.

ALWAYS HAVE GOOD INTENTIONS
www.franklinspeaksup.com

MAKE CHANGES

You don't have to debate or remember the truth.

Educators teach,
so ask questions.

MAKE CHANGES

Understanding is the process of asking the question over and over again until you understand.

MAKE CHANGES

Your lies, your hate, your drama all belong to you.

MAKE CHANGES

You are not required to help in any way.

Take the time to understand why you are the way you are, then change?

The library is a free resource.

MAKE CHANGES

Save yourself first!

MAKE CHANGES

Read Make Changes over and over again until you see a positive shift in you.

The good news will show up.

MAKE CHANGES

You should be very proud of yourself.

Now Make Changes.

MAKE CHANGES

In Closing,

I want to thank you for purchasing Make Changes as a gift for someone you care about, or for your own personal journey.

Always remember TRUST is stronger than distrust, and RESPECT is stronger than envy.

I look forward to your feedback.

With all my care and love for your well-being,
Franklin

Made in the USA
Middletown, DE
18 June 2023